Nothing Lasts Forever

Roman Pompeii

ONE UNIT IN THE
SPINDLE STORIES
WOMEN'S WORLD HISTORY SERIES

Lyn Reese

Copyright © 1990
Women In World History Curriculum
1030 Spruce Street
Berkeley, CA 94707
510-524-0304

Acknowledgments
Editors:
    Dr. Mary Agnes Dougherty
    Jean Benson Wilkinson
Illustrator:
    Nancy Gorell
Layout Consultant:
    Charles Reese
Classroom Field Test:
    Tess Henry

Spindle Stories

Other Units in the Spindle Stories Series

Women In World History Curriculum

1030 Spruce Street
Berkeley, California 94707
510-524-0304
FAX 510-524-0112
Web Site: www.WomenInWorldHistory.com

ISBN 0-9625880-5-9

KEY CONCEPTS

EVERYDAY LIFE IN A ROMAN TOWN

WOMEN'S ROLES IN RELIGIONS

THE RELATIONSHIP OF WOMEN TO ROMAN POLITICAL STRUCTURES

ECONOMIC CONTRIBUTIONS OF DIFFERENT CLASSES OF WOMEN

EXPECTED BEHAVIOR OF ROMAN MATRONS

OBJECTS AND LOCATIONS THAT HELP IDENTIFY WOMEN'S LIVES

RIGHTS OF WOMEN IN GREECE AND IN ROME

TABLE OF CONTENTS

PREFACE

This book is one unit in the series: **Spindle Stories, Women's World History**. The series is called Spindle Stories because the spindle is a universal symbol of womankind. Within most cultures, the spinning of wool, flax, cotton and silk traditionally has been a woman's task. Throughout the centuries images, artifacts, poems, folk tales, songs, and goddesses dedicated to the art of spinning, reveal the importance of this task in women's lives. In the Dark Ages, for example, spindle whorls, the weight that pulls the spindle down while it is turning, were found buried with each female. When you pick up a spindle, thousands of years of women's history rest in your hands!

While there is reference to women's essential work in cloth production in most of the **Spindle Stories** books, this is *not* their focus. Each book instead offers original stories and follow-up activities as a way of presenting history from the female perspective. They show how women, the majority of humankind, have been essential to the making of history.

The books present the life experiences of diverse women from the few who are well-known to the lesser known majority. Readers will learn of women who were farmers, artisans, healers, writers, entertainers, religious leaders, managers, and traders. They will see where women held power and where they did not. They will learn that women's political and economic functions and their status and rights varied according to time and place, and could change over time.

The original stories usually recount the adventures of a young woman on the verge of adulthood. Accompanying each story are multi-level, multi-discipline activity sheets. An essay and selected bibliography are provided offering additional information on the history of women in the period. For easy reading, the stories are divided into two parts with follow-up discussion questions. For the classroom, either part I or II of the stories plus an activity might be assigned as homework.

Nothing Lasts Forever

PART I. The Mountain Giants are Restless:

Down, down the steep, narrow path Cornelia ran. Her breath was short and she heard her heart beat in time with the pounding of her feet. Pushing aside tired farmers who were returning from a day's selling in the city, she sped on. Thoughts of the past hours crowded her mind. She had spent far too long visiting her nursemaid's elderly mother, Nonia. She had enjoyed far too much the afternoon spent among the grape vines ripening on the slopes of Mt. Vesuvius. Listening to Nonia's stories of her childhood in Syria, Cornelia had lost track of the time. Now she would be missed at home. She hurried on.

Nonia was an ex-slave who had been able to buy her freedom five years ago. She was living her last days simply on the mountain. Aurelia was Nonia's daughter and Cornelia's nursemaid. She was still a slave. Aurelia knew that Cornelia loved the mountain. So she let Cornelia slip away whenever her tutor, Lyturcus the Greek, was ill, or whenever her mother was too busy to give Cornelia her daily weaving lessons. Cornelia knew that Aurelia spoiled her because her own children had been sold away from her when they were babies. Cornelia had become like Aurelia's own child. Cornelia often felt that she had two mothers instead of one!

Cornelia made herself think about the path and getting home. Now it was late and Aurelia would be angry at her absence. Maybe Cornelia's mother would learn about these little visits and then both child and slave would be punished and it would be her fault. Cornelia became angry with herself. She knew it was time to move away from childish pleasures such as these mountain visits. Soon she would enter her mother's religion in a formal initiation ceremony. Shortly after that she would be married. A Roman matron with grown up duties did not go about without an escort, as Cornelia had done today. She did not slip away from her home and her duties.

Dust from the dry August earth rose in small puffs as Cornelia's feet beat against the dirt. Lifting her dark eyes she caught the glints of the late afternoon sun on the water of the bay. Two trading ships were slowly gliding into the port, the galley slaves beating their oars in rhythm to move the ships along. "Probably bringing in grain from Spain or precious papyrus from Egypt," thought Cornelia. She stopped for a moment to catch her breath and looked away from the ships, back at her beloved mountain covered with leafy green terraces of wine grapes and groves of olive and fruit trees. Although strange rumblings lately had been heard coming from deep within the mountain, Cornelia smiled warmly and thought, "Fruit and beauty are the harvest of my mountain, not grain and paper."

With its tiled roofed houses and stone streets laid out in a regular pattern, Pompeii lay just below her. Cornelia could just make out the shape of the wide outdoor forum, and she imagined the colorful awnings that covered the stalls of the open market in the middle. She saw the tops of the plane trees that lined the open gymnasium and swimming pool, and the large oval shape of the stone amphitheater. Thanks to the late Emperor Augustus' decree allowing women to attend, she could now go there to join the rowdy crowds that cheered the bloody gladiator and wild beast contests.

Cornelia was a strong runner. Her dark curls bounced against her face as she raced past the fields of sweet flowers that Pompeians grew to make perfume and to decorate their homes. She finally reached the East Gate and there entered the town through the walls. Since the peace of the Emperor Augustus these protective walls weren't needed, but they did serve to separate the life of the country from that of the city. Inside the walls, the smells of the city made Cornelia's nose tingle. On one side of the street a snack bar sold cheese, sausages and fragrant round bread. Across the narrow street a workshop was brewing Pompeii's famous but strong smelling fish sauce. Directly before her, a flock of musty, fat sheep, newly brought from the market, blocked her way. Cornelia deftly jumped between them, avoiding the garbage on the street by using the stepping stones laid across the streets to keep people away from the refuse.

Weaving through the afternoon crowds, Cornelia was almost home when, rounding a corner, she was stopped by a procession of gladiators on their way from their barracks to the amphitheater. To let them go by, Cornelia flattened herself against the wall of one of the houses that lined the narrow street. The late afternoon sun glittered on the gladiators' vizored helmets and polished headdresses. One Cornelia recognized as a current favorite. He had managed to survive by vigorously defeating many opponents. He walked separately from the others carrying his finely decorated plumed helmet and short sword, gifts from one of his patrons. His eyes arrogantly searched each passerby, seemingly to say, "I may be about to die, but I am better and braver than you!" Cornelia turned her eyes away and concentrated instead on reading the latest graffiti (writings) on the wall of the house across the street: *"Samius to*

Cornelius: go hang yourself!" "If anyone lost a mare with a small pack saddle let him come and see Quintus Decium Hilarus!" "There is no room for loafers here - move on!" Then one message caught her eye and tightened her heart. It was a poem which ended, *"Nothing can last forever."* Cornelia wondered, "Is this meant for me to read now when I'm face to face with a procession of men who are meant to fight and die, *and* at such a disturbing time in my life? Then there is Mount Vesuvius! Nonia told me again today of the story of its mountain giants. Even though they were defeated years ago by the gods and imprisoned under the mountain, sometimes the giants struggle to get out. When they do the earth moves and walls and buildings fall. Does this message have anything to do with Vesuvius' recent tremblings? Are they caused by the struggles of the mountain giants? Now I have many things on my mind - men who must die, growing up, and restless giants!"

An Unfinished Argument: Pushing aside these thoughts, Cornelia at last could go on her way. Soon she reached the bright blue-plastered stone walls of her home. It was a house that reflected the success of her businessman father, Cornelius Marcus Porcius. His two fullers (cleaning and wool dyeing businesses) were doing well. One was managed by the woman, Specle. Both shops were kept busy cleaning the white togas that all well-to-do men who were Roman citizens were required to wear.

Cornelia greeted the doorman and entered directly into the home's atrium (open courtyard). In this part of the house the rooms were filled with sunlight and Cornelia felt that she was back in the country. The sun shone on the wall paintings

of scenes from country life and of stories about gods and goddesses. Its rays sparkled on the mosaics (small colored tiles) fashioned in the shape of fish and shells that covered the floors. The wide atrium was filled with flowers, a gushing fountain and a fish pond. The water was brought by the aqueduct which came down to Pompeii from Abellinum, almost 15 miles away. Cornelia heard a deep voice boom out, "Salve lucrum" (welcome earnings). That was her father's bookkeeper. An educated slave, he was welcoming a client in the tablinum (reception room).

Cornelia quickly left the atrium and moved to the women's section. It was a smaller, darker and less airy part of the house. In the tiny kitchen some of the household's 25 slaves bustled about preparing the dinner. Two women were busy lifting a heavy frying pan to the bronze stove. In it simmered a fish stew in a spicy sauce. Others were taking clay pots filled with meat out of the hearth; another was pouring oil from an amphora (large jar). Aurelia was cutting up lettuce and leeks for a salad. She immediately spotted Cornelia. "As usual you are

late. I don't know why I let you do things on your own. But look at you! Your face is as flushed as a pomegranate. Too much sun, no doubt - and maybe a fever!" At this thought Aurelia's voice raised in alarm and she immediately called the household doctor. She quickly discovered that Cornelia indeed had a fever. Dosed with herbal medicine, Cornelia was put to bed on her couch in her small dark bedroom.

Sleep was almost upon Cornelia when she heard her parents' voices. The two had just entered the peristyle (second courtyard) near Cornelia's room. Here they often came to admire the garden while they waited for their dinner. Tonight, the chill in their voices matched the cool evening breeze that stirred their robes. "Perhaps this is not the best time for Cornelia's initiation into the temple of Isis," began her father cautiously. "She seems unusually flustered lately, out of harmony with things. Perhaps you should wait until spring. In the meantime we have to remember that she's almost 13 years old and it's time she takes a husband. She's beginning to be noticed, with her smooth olive skin, brooding eyes and curling hair. And she's strong and straight and healthy. Yes, it's time."

Cornelia crept out of bed and put her ear against the wall so she could hear better. Her father, too, had noticed that she was growing up! Cornelia's father paused, but as there was no answer from her mother he continued. "Since we want her to contract a free marriage, so that I may continue as her guardian and watch over her property, we need time to work one out. Maybe you'd consider young Stehanus Florian. I saw him at the bath trying to perfect his boxing skills. Although he's not much of an athlete, his family estate is doing well and..." Now Cornelia's mother spoke and she clearly was upset. "I cannot let you interfere with Cornelia's initiation into the Isis cult at this late stage! I don't know why you even bring it up! There have been careful preparations for her and I can only believe that you are opposed to them."

"You know that my family has always worshiped Minerva and Mithras, my patron God when I was with the army," asserted her father. "Since women cannot worship in Mithras' temple, I know you cannot love him. But Minerva is patroness of my business and important to us. It is Minerva who has given our family success in our business, not the goddess Isis! Surely you should pay more attention to

4

Minerva! I also wonder if you shouldn't be making sure that Cornelia is better versed in the ceremonies offered to our Emperor, rather than those offered to a goddess whom people from the sordid lands of Egypt have always worshipped!" Cornelia wanted to listen to her parents, but at the same time she wished she couldn't hear them argue.

"You and your family know perfectly well that I always do my public duty to the Emperor and to your family's Lares (household gods)," continued her mother, still agitated. "The shrines are well kept, and I have taught the children their correct duties to them. I think you resent the fact that Isis has spoken directly to me and has asked me to help others to learn of her promise of life after death. She has raised me to a position of importance at the temple that I can't refuse." Cornelia's father replied, "Yes, yes, you can be a priestess if you wish, but I am uncomfortable about our daughter! I don't mind what happens in the privacy of the temple, but those long processions you're involved in through the forum and the market and gates. They're attended more and more, it seems, by sailors from the East, slaves from parts I barely know, and women of bad reputation. Who knows, next you may be looking into that new ridiculous Eastern sect I heard of called Christianity. Cornelia must appear respectable before everyone if we're to contract the best marriage for her."

This tension between her parents was not new. In the end, Cornelia knew that her mother would win. Her importance to the temple of Isis, "Oh mother of a thousand names be blessed," was too great. And, her father had no reason to find fault with her mother's duties at home, religious or otherwise. She managed the slaves with a perfect touch. She was a clever buyer at the shops. She was not overly friendly with other men, was obedient much of the time, and her spinning skills were unsurpassed. She even had some education and could converse well at dinner parties. She was, in short, the ideal Roman matron!

Cornelia and her two brothers were proud of their mother. They knew that their mother found comfort in the fact that the Goddess Isis herself had lost a child. Cornelia's mother had lost three children, two boys and a girl - all when they were babies. They knew their mother also liked the goddess' promise to make women equal to men. Her eyes had gleamed when she had taught them the prayer that said, "Oh Isis, you who gave women power equal with men!" And then there were the ceremonies for Isis, such as the Feast of the Ships, that they all enjoyed - even her father. During that festival, all the ships which had been brought ashore or stranded during the year were repaired, blessed and sent to sea again. Yes, her mother would win this debate and Cornelia would move one step closer to womanhood and one more step away from the delicious, spur-of-the-moment visits to the mountain. Yet, the afternoon's visit stayed with her as she dozed off - a memory that burned as bright in her heart as the fever burned in her head.

Use the story to answer these questions:

1) *Were there any jobs that slaves did in Pompeii that surprised you? Name them. Name the other work that slaves performed. Why do you think that there were many slaves in Roman Pompeii?*

2) *Find out who the Emperor Augustus was. What was the "peace of Augustus" that he imposed? How would such a peace help the citizens of Pompeii? What right had the emperor given to the women of Pompeii?*

3) *Name some things that a well-to-do or free woman in Pompeii could do to achieve respect? What things could a man do to achieve respect?*

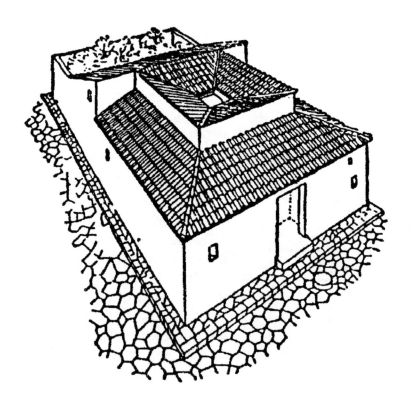

PART II. The Dancing Walls:

Light from the early morning sun filtered into Cornelia's room, waking her. She knew at once that she felt better. Although the servants had been up since before dawn, Cornelia managed to slip out of bed unnoticed. She quietly washed her face and took a drink from the running water brought in by lead pipes buried under the city streets. Grabbing a handful of figs and honey balls left over from last night's supper, she slipped unnoticed out the trades people's door at the back of the house. She had a plan for the day! She would be a carefree girl, just a little longer.

"Maybe this will be the last time I can wander on my own," she thought. "I want so much to see my best friend Julia. She will be married next month and will leave for an estate near the great capital of Rome. I must see her now, before we next meet as matrons. Then our lives will be busy, full of the duties of our new household."

Julia's family was very rich, richer than Cornelia's. They lived in a huge estate outside the city walls. The walk was long, and the day already had grown overcast. Luckily, Cornelia knew how to avoid those streets bustling with slaves and farmers buying goods, and those with public fountains where women from poor families collected water. She also was far away from the public forum where men gathered to argue over politics and legal matters or to bargain at the slave market. She did, however, have to pass by the gambling houses and taverns which even in this early hour were occupied. Out of the dark interior of a gambling house a scowling man stumbled, knocking into Cornelia. He was a large odd looking man, with a scraggly beard and hair the color of gold. "Sorry, sorry, but this is not my day, little one," he mumbled in broken Latin. "Fate rules the earth and it and the stars have decreed my downfall in Pompeii - I've lost all my money." At the word Pompeii, as if to echo his black thoughts, the earth gave a small tremble. "That decides it, I'm off to my ship. I hope my master will bring us out of this sea and home to Briton," said the foreigner. Darting a worried glance at the mountain looming above the city, he hurried off.

The earth's tremor had upset Cornelia too. Her mood darkened as she left the city through the large gate that led to the nearby city of Herculaneum. She felt uneasy as she made her way past the large stone tombs that lined the sides of the road. Since it was forbidden to bury the dead within the city gates, the roads leading to Pompeii were lined with these large stone monuments. Normally Cornelia did not fear the tombs. She enjoyed the yearly feast held at her family's tomb. She often went with her father to help tend the big, beautiful tomb the red headed priestess and wealthy patroness of the

LIVIA
WIFE OF CORNELIVS
SHE KEPT THE HOVSE
AND WORKED IN WOOL

Fullers Guild, Eumachia, had built for herself. Today, however, the tombs loomed large and unfriendly. To Cornelia, they seemed a warning to the travelers hurrying past - *"Nothing can last forever."* To give herself courage, Cornelia clutched at the bulla (leather charm) given to her on her naming day, the 8th day of her life. On the day she was married she would have to give up her bulla and all her childhood toys. But for the moment, it hung safely around her neck.

There was more activity than usual when she reached Julia's beautiful villa which sat high on a small hill overlooking the sea. Horses and carts filled with wooden inlaid tables, bronze furniture and even some of the villa's marble statues rumbled past. "Julia's inside," she was told. "We are removing some of the household items to our other country house to protect it from the shaking of the earth," explained a servant.

Inside the villa things were more peaceful. Searching for her friend, Cornelia walked through the many rooms that led into other rooms. Suddenly her head began to pound. "Oh, no, not again," she thought, recognizing that her sickness and fever had returned. Catching hold of a doorway, she stumbled into a darkened room. To ease her head, she lay on the tile floor on her back, eyes closed. After a few minutes, she opened her eyes ever so slowly. As they focused in the dark, Cornelia realized with a shock that she was not alone. Above her head, around the walls of the dark room, strange people appeared - people who seemed to float in space. "Who are you? Do I know you? I am Cornelia, named after Cornelius, the fuller merchant." Cornelia found herself whispering these words over and over again. No one answered. One woman carrying a plate of olives silently glared down at her. She seemed to say, "Be quiet you fool; you don't belong here." Behind her, the wall dripped a color of red. Was it blood?

Cornelia lay stone still, barely breathing. To her left, above her, was a young woman who seemed to be listening to words read to her from a special scroll. Next to them, another woman, cloak flung behind her, was warding off some unknown force - was it evil? Cornelia then saw a kneeling figure about to uncover a mysterious object covered in purple. "Where am I," thought Cornelia, "at a sacred ceremony? I really shouldn't be here." She saw a torch which seemed to shine over the scene revealing another woman with a raised whip. "Oh gods and goddesses, she is going to strike that woman," cried out Cornelia. Yet her voice did not rise above a whisper. No one seemed to hear her. The woman, awaiting her punishment, lay across the lap of a friend. Surprisingly she seemed to accept her fate. Indeed the room seemed to be filled with joy. Cornelia noticed a woman who was dancing gaily to the sound of cymbals. She saw black winged gods and goddesses

wearing masks. Some played music. "But why can't I hear anything and why can't they hear me? Does this scene foretell of my own initiation? Am I dreaming, or is this real?" Her head spun and swirled, and the colors mixed and deepened as the mute voices and music called out their silent rhythms. Clutching her head, Cornelia cried out in anguish and fainted as though she were drugged.

The Snake Bracelet: A soothing voice and cool cloth on her forehead woke Cornelia from her deep sleep. "You're home now, your fever has gone," Aurelia was telling her. "You were found on the floor of the room where Julia's mother had painted a real life picture of people being initiated into the temple of Dionysus. No one knows how you got there and your family accepts the idea that you didn't know what you were doing because of your fever." At that moment Cornelia's mother swept into the room, now fully in charge. "Young woman, you will stay with me, under my wing from now on. And our first task is to get you clean. Off to the baths." Fine, it was off to the baths for Cornelia who was stiff and weak from this illness that came and went. She was perfectly happy to obey.

When the gongs announced that the furnaces were lit to heat the water, the women of Procius family set forth. They were armed with rolled white towels and fragrant oils, and accompanied by slaves holding umbrellas to shade them from the sun. Entering the women's section of their favorite bath, Cornelia quickly shed her clothes, entered first the frigidarium (cold bath) and then the tempidarium (warm bath). She ended her cleaning with a dip in the calidarium (hot bath).

As she dried herself Cornelia could hear men's voices over the wall. They were in their sports field and separate gymnasium area. Usually she harbored a wish that the women too could have a playing field for themselves. But today she was content to sit quietly, watching and learning from the women at the baths. Early in her life she had been taught the importance of becoming an obedient and proper young Roman woman. Nevertheless, Cornelia learned different messages from the women she saw at the baths. Here, as they soaked in the water, relaxed under a gentle massage, or played their favorite knucklebone games, other matters were discussed. Although the women had no say in public matters, they certainly had opinions. Sometimes, it seemed, the women were most concerned about laws which forbid them to display their wealth. In the past, women who wore expensive jewelry or fine clothes had been taxed. With all the beautiful

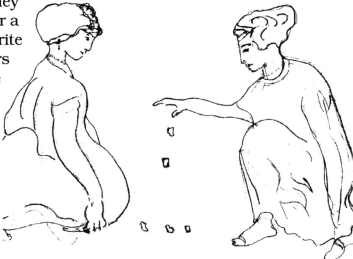

possessions these women wore, Cornelia could see that a special tax on women could be worrisome.

Cornelia let her thoughts wander to recent events in her own life. It occurred to her that any new step, such as her coming initiation and then her marriage, had both a good and bad side. There was both joy and pain in the process of growing. She thought about the stirrings deep inside her mountain. "Maybe the rumblings are not the awakening of giants, maybe the mountain is reflecting my mood, my uneasiness." She thought about her fear of the paintings on the villa's walls. "Perhaps Isis is displeased with me because I am fearful of joining her attendants." Cornelia made up her mind. "Today I shall please the goddess; I'll join the afternoon worship and bring an offering of perfume to ask her favors."

Cornelia's mother was pleased with her daughter's request to visit Isis and announced that they all should go. Calling two slaves to attend her, she began the lengthy job of readying herself to leave the baths. One slave applied white chalk power to her face, red rouge to her cheeks, and layers of eye makeup. Another slave pinned on her stola (long, colored sleeveless tunic), worn only by proper Roman matrons. Finally, the blond wig made of hair brought from Germanic tribes far to the north, was settled on her head. It was held in place with a gold band. Her jewelry today consisted only of pearl and emerald drop earrings and a single gold arm bracelet fashioned like a snake - a symbol which represented Isis. Cornelia's mother looked at the bracelet for awhile. Then, on an impulse, she slipped it off her arm and offered it to Cornelia. "Take this as a sign of my pleasure in the fact that you are growing up. Soon you'll be initiated into the temple and someday you and I may be priestesses together. Let this sign of Isis show you how much I care for you and how eagerly I look forward to that day." Cornelia's eyes filled with tears as she accepted the gift and slid it on her arm. She did not say a word, but she knew that her mother understood how she felt.

Wrapping their palla (outer cloaks) tightly about them, the women of the Procius family then hurried into the street. As they reached the walls surrounding the temple of Isis, Cornelia stopped and looked up toward Mt. Vesuvius. The words from the wall graffiti again came to her. "Nothing can last forever," she mouthed as she looked toward the mountain. "You know," she thought, " for me this really has turned out to be true. I wonder if it applies to mountain giants as well?" Touching her new bracelet, she turned and followed her mother into the grounds of the peaceful temple.

Epilogue: The giants of Mount Vesuvius soon gave Cornelia their answer. With a deafening roar, in August 79 A.D. the whole top of the mountain blew open in an enormous explosion. Searing flames soared high into the sky. Cinders shot forth creating an immense black cloud which covered the land - even to the tops of the trees. Molten rock and mud spewed down the mountain. Pompeii, lying below the peak, was covered with cinders and poisonous gasses. Cornelia, her family, her house, and her city were rapidly buried under the volcanic debris.

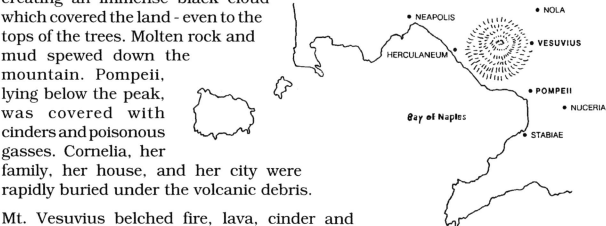

Mt. Vesuvius belched fire, lava, cinder and gasses for three days. The city was covered so completely that it was perfectly preserved and soon people forgot that it had been there. It was nearly two thousand years before the city of Pompeii, Cornelia's once civilized and beautiful world, was discovered and uncovered by archeologists again.

11

Use the story to answer these questions:

1) What types of buildings did archaeologists find when they uncovered Pompeii? How do you think a volcanic eruption can preserve a whole town?

2) Name some ways free women in Pompeii made money. How do you know that Eumachia, the patroness of the Fullers Guild, was wealthy?

3) If Cornelia had lived, in a short time she would have become an adult. What are some things she would have done to show that she no longer was a child?

4) Do we have initiation ceremonies today? Have you ever participated in one? Was there anything mysterious about the ceremony? Did the initiation help you feel you were more a part of the group you were joining?

Terms to Help You Understand the Story

Amphitheater: A round or oval building with rising rows of seats around an open space where sports events, etc. are held.

Epilogue: A comment by the author added at the end of a story or play.

Forum: A public meeting place where lawmakers and courts met.

Initiation: A special ceremony some clubs, organizations, or religions require of new members.

Galley: A large, low ship with both sails and oars. Usually slaves or prisoners in chains rowed the ship.

Gladiator: A slave or captive who fought against animals or others for the entertainment of the public. Usually they fought until one of the contestants was killed.

Guardian: A person who takes charge of an other person, often a child, who is not allowed to handle their own affairs.

Matron: A older married or widowed woman.

Papyrus: A kind of writing paper made from a tall plant which grew in or near water.

Pomegranate: A round, red fruit with a hard skin and many seeds.

Terraces: Flat platforms of earth which rise, one above the other, on a hillside. Terraces are necessary for crops which are planted on steep slopes.

Follow Up Worksheet

1) Pretend you are an "archeologist" who has been digging into the ruins of Pompeii. You are interested in finding out about how women lived. You have found a gold arm bracelet fashioned like a snake and a journal, written on papyrus, that described the last days of a young woman called Cornelia. Describe at least four objects and places you will now try to look for to learn about the lives of Roman women. Explain what each place or object could tell us.

_____

_____

_____

_____

_____

_____

_____

2) Find three examples from the story that describe how Cornelia is expected to behave as a Roman matron.

_____

_____

_____

Put a star next to those behaviors that seem similar to how young women in the United States are expected to behave today.

3) List three ways you think young men might have been expected to behave in Pompeii. Select one that might still be true today.

_____

_____

_____

4) List three things Cornelia could do that a female slave could not.

_____

_____

_____

5) Give two reasons why the cult of Isis appealed to Cornelia's mother?

_____

_____

Research: Find out about Mithras and why this cult appealed to Roman soldiers. Why couldn't women join the cult?

6) Many women's tombstones in Roman times said that the woman "kept the house and worked in wool." What did this mean?

_____

_____

_____

LIVIA
WIFE OF CORNELIVS
SHE KEPT THE HOVSE
AND WORKED IN WOOL

If you were to write an inscription for a plaque that could be used to describe women today, what would you say?

_____

_____

_____

POMPEII 79 A.D.

1) Locate the following sites in Pompeii by using the legend. Answer the True/False questions by using the legend and information in the story.

- Pompeii had more than one bakery.   ___True   ___False

- Cornelia passed the tomb of Eumenchia on her way to Julia's house.

  ___True   ___False

- Most of the temples were near the Forum.   ___True   ___False

- The closet gate to Pompeii's port was on the north side.   ___True   ___False

- From their barracks, the gladiators passed Cornelia's house to get to the amphitheater.   ___True   ___False

- There were only a few places of entertainment in Pompeii.

  ___True   ___False

- Men had more places to bathe than women.   ___True   ___False

2) Describe how each site was used.
   Use your textbook for information if you are unsure.

3) Trace one route Cornelia might have taken from her house to Julia's. Use information in the story for clues.

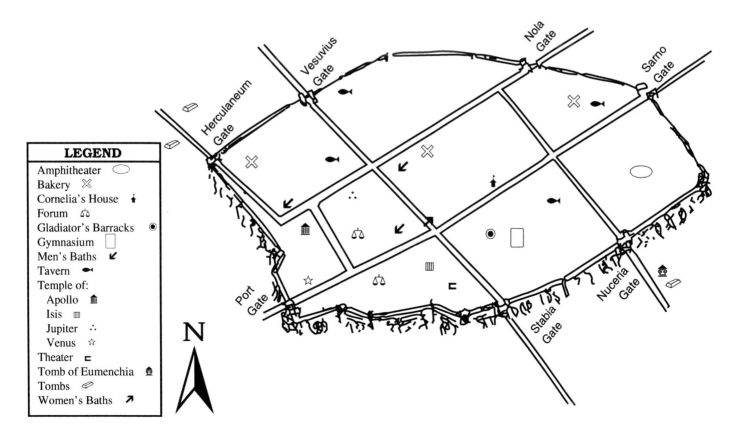

LEGEND

Amphitheater	⬭
Bakery	✖
Cornelia's House	✝
Forum	⚖
Gladiator's Barracks	◉
Gymnasium	☐
Men's Baths	↙
Tavern	➤
Temple of:	
Apollo	🏛
Isis	⬚
Jupiter	∴
Venus	☆
Theater	⊏
Tomb of Eumenchia	🏮
Tombs	▱
Women's Baths	↗

N

TEMPLE OF ISIS

National Geographic Reproduction in L. Green, "Isis: The Egyptian goddess Who Endured in the Graeco Roman World," K.M.T.: A Modern Journal of Ancient Egypt, vol. 5, Winter, 1994-1995.

Finding Clues
What Do Images Tell Us?

Pretend that you are an archeologist in Pompeii who has uncovered the images shown on pages 2 and 3. Some are carved on walls or tombs, some are statues, some are painted on walls. Study them, looking for clues about what they can tell us about women.

Suggested Activities

1) Make a list of what you can see for at least one of these topics.
   - Types of clothes women wore
   - Types of hair styles
   - Tasks women did

2) Choose one image. Brainstorm descriptive words about the person or persons in the picture. What was the person doing? How did the person (s) look? Was the person poor or rich? How might the person feel at this moment? Put words in the person's mouth. What might she be saying? Tell what you think the woman is going to do next.

3) Compare portraits numbers (3) and (5). What might these two women say to each other? Have anything in common with each other?

4) Select one image. Looking at it, write some questions to ask the person. What you would like to know about this person if she could answer you? What more do you need to know to understand what this person's life was really like?

5) Put the images in any order that tells a dramatic story, or a funny cartoon. Put words in each person's mouth.

6) Choose any item of clothing or ornamentation from the images. Replicate it by drawing. Display.

7) Looking again at the map of Pompeii, select at least four of the images and tell where you think the archeologist might have found them. Why might these paintings or statues have been put there? Why were they made? Why do you think this person(s) became the subject of this piece of art?

(1) PHYSICIAN DISPENSING MEDICINES

(2) BOYS AND GIRLS PLAYING A GAME TOGETHER

(3) SCHOLAR

(4) MIDWIFE ASSISTING AT BIRTH

(5) SLAVE GRINDING GRAIN

(6) POURING PERFUME

(7) Priestesses and Priests bringing offerings to Goddess Isis

(8) Statue of Eumachia

(10) A wedding - groom holds marriage contract

(9) Butcher in her shop

(11) Woman being prepared by servants

Finding Clues
What Do Writers Tell Us?

Your task is to match the following quotes by Roman writers to the images on the previous two pages. After you select the quote, place its number next to the picture. Not all the quotes will exactly fit the image; select the one that works the best.

When you finish matching the quotes to the images, chose one quote that interests you. Does your quote offer a positive or negative opinion about women? Explain.

1) "It is good for the midwife to able to see the face of the mother, so she can calm her fears and assure her that there is nothing to worry about and the childbirth is going well...She should take care that the infant not fall out at once. When the infant tries to come out, the midwife should have a cloth in her hands to pick him up."
   - *Instruction for the Midwife, Rome, 1st century*

2) "The least respectable of all trades are those which minister to pleasure...fishmongers, butchers, cooks, sausage-makers. Add to these, if you like, perfumers, dancers, and actors."
   - *Cicero*

3) "I am Mother Nature, the universal mother, mistress of all the elements, queen of the living and the dead...Every people knows me by their own name: Artemis, Aphrodite, Persephone, Demeter, Hecate. But those who live in Egypt and those who dwell far to the East, understand my ancient wisdom more than any others, for they know the ceremonies that are dear to me and call me by my true name - Almighty Isis."
   - *Lucius Apuleius reporting on what he claimed the goddess told him in a vision*

4) "Pamphile was a learned woman. She wrote historical memoirs in thirty-three books, and many other books, about controversies, and many other things."
   - *From The Suda, an Ancient book, 1st century.*

5) "A suitable person...must be respectable since people will have to trust the secrets of their lives to her and because to women of bad character the semblance of medical instruction is a cover for evil scheming...She will be free from superstition so as not to overlook salutary measures on account of a dream or omen or some customary rite or vulgar superstition."
   - *Soranus on training of a female doctor. 2nd century.*

6) "To Dmois, worn out by her work; beloved by the household that raised her. When she died she received this monument."
   - *Roman Athens, 2nd/3rd century*

7) "It should be the same with married people - a mutual blending of bodies, property, friends and relations. Indeed what the Roman lawgiver had in mind...was to make man and wife feel that everything belonged to both of them together."
   - *Advice on Marriage. Plutarch, 2nd century*

8) "Eumachia, daughter of Lucius, public priestess, the fullers dedicated this statue."
   - *Pompeii Fuller Union*

9) "Parents don't bring their children up in the way of decency and discipline but in a willful way and without manners. The result is that the children gradually learn to be cheeky and show no respect either for themselves or others."
   - *Tacitus, Roman historian*

10) "The right scent for a woman is none at all."
    - *Plautus.*

11) "If you saw women getting out of bed in the morning, you would find them more repulsive than monkeys. ...A troupe of servants surround her plastering her unhappy face with a variety of medications...Innumerable salves are used to brighten her complexion. As in a public procession, each of the servants has some different object in her hand, enough to stock a chemist's shop, jars full of mischief."
    - *Lucian*

Plate decorated with fish popular in Roman times.
(Italy between 350-300 B.C.)

Let's Cook - Let's Eat!
Roman Recipes

On a typical day Cornelia woke up at dawn and ate only a light breakfast of bread and honey. She ate her main meal with her parents in late afternoon. Their dining room, called the *triclinium*, was filled with three couches rather than chairs since it was considered elegant to eat lying on one's side. The couches surrounded the table, or *mensa*. In contrast, the kitchen was a small, poorly lit room. Here mostly slaves cooked over smoky fires.

MATRON BUYING A GOOSE

Like other well-off families in Pompeii, Cornelia's parents often gave dinner parties. Some were great banquets which started early in the afternoon and ran well into the evening. Cornelia's mother mainly was in charge of these affairs. She had to make sure the proper social standing of each guest was respected, that they were not placed next to someone of lower rank. Both she and Cornelia's father had to circulate among their guests to make sure everyone was happy.

One Roman writer, Sallust, praised a good hostess when he said, "She possessed intellectual strengths which are by no means laughable...cracking jokes, speaking either modestly or tenderly or saucily - in a word, she had much wit!"

Another writer, Juvenal, made fun of the female guest "who begs as soon as she sits down to dinner, to discourse on poets and poetry, comparing Virgil with Homer. Professors, critics, lawyers, auctioneers - even another woman - can't get a word in. She rattles on at such a rate that you'd think all the pots and pans in the kitchen were crashing to the floor or that every bell in town was clanging."

PLAN OF POMPEIAN HOUSE

Bedroom

Bedroom

Triclinium

Penstyle

Kitchen

Tablinum

Bedroom

Bedroom

Bedroom

Atrium

Porter's room

Shop

Shop

Here are some recipes to try taken from an old Roman cookbook. The cooking temperatures and times haven't been handed down in all cases, but you should be able to figure out how to cook them. Each serves four people.

ISICIA OMENTATA - Burgers
Ingredients

3/4th pound minced meat
1 french roll, soaked in unsweetened white grape juice
1/2 tsp. freshly ground pepper
1/2 tsp salt
some pine nuts and green peppercorns
baking foil

Mix minced meat with the soaked french roll. Mix the ground spices into the meat. Form small burgers and put pine nuts and peppercorns into them. Put them on baking foil and grill them.

FABACIAE VIRIDES - Green Beans
Ingredients

3/4 pound green beans
1/2 tsp salt with 10 tblsp white grape juice
1-2 tblsp of oil
1/1 tblsp ground coriander seed
1 tsp cumin seeds
1/2 minced leek

Cook beans with salted grape juice, oil, leek and spices. Serve.

MUSTACEI - Rolls
Ingredients

1 pound wheat flour
1 cup white grape juice
2 tblsp anise seeds
a tblsp cumin seeds
3.5 ounces lard, or butter
2 ounces grated cheese (sheep's cheese would be best)
about 20 bay leaves

Poor some grape juice over the flour, (Use yeast dough or add 2 ounces of yeast to the flour and grape juice. Leave it a while to rise). Add anise and cumin seeds, the lard and cheese. Work it together until you have a reasonable dough. Form rolls, then put one bay leaf under each roll.
Bake 30-35 minutes at 350 F.

PULLIS FUSILIS - Chicken with filling
Ingredients

1 fresh chicken
3/4th minced meat (half beef, half pork)
3.5 ounces oats
2 eggs
1 cup white grape juice
1 tblsp oil
1/4 tps ground ginger
1/4 ground pepper
1 tsp peppercorns
1 ounce pine nuts
salt to taste

Mix pepper, ginger, minced meat and cooked oats. Add eggs and mix until you have a smooth mass. Add oil, whole peppercorns and pine nuts. Fill this dough into the chicken. Cook approximately 1 hour at 400 degrees in the oven.

PATINA DE PIRIS - Pear Souffle
Ingredients
2.2 pounds pears (peeled and without the core)
6 eggs
4 tblsp honey
7 tblsp sweetened grape juice.
    (First boil a cup of white grape juice with some honey.
    Reduce it to half.
    From this mixture measure out your 7 tblsp.)
a little bit of oil
1/4 salt
1/2 ground cumin
ground pepper to taste

Mesh cooked and peeled pears (without core) together with pepper, cumin, honey, grape juice and oil. Add eggs and put into a casserole. Cook approximately 30 minutes on low to moderate heat. Serve with a bit of pepper sprinkled on the souffle.

DULCIA DOMESTICA - Housemade Dessert
Ingredients
1/2 pound fresh or dried dates
2 ounces coarsely ground nuts
a little bit of salt
some red grape juice
honey

Take pits out of the dates and fill them with nuts. Sprinkle a bit of salt on the filled dates and stew them in honey-sweetened red grape juice. The dates have to be cooked on low heat until their skins start to come off. (approximately 5-10 minutes).

Recipes taken and modified from "Antique Roman Dishes - Collection" by Micaela Pantke. WEB site:
http://www.mit.edu:8001/people/wchuang/cooking/recipes/Roman/Ancient_Roman.html.

Tools Uncover Women's Work

Research: What if in the ruins of Pompeii you came upon these two objects. Someone tells you that they are important tools women have used for thousands of years. Do you know what they are? If not, use the following clues to help you find out.

1) The tools are used together.

2) Women have used them to produce clothes, bed coverings, rugs, wall hangings, tents and even sails for ships.

3) Your mother's side of your family is called the "distaff side." Look up this term to help you in your research.

4) These tools were so commonly used by Roman women, that a well known poet, Catullus, in 54 B.C. wrote a poem about them. The poem names the tools and describes how they were used. Read it, and then name the tools. Can you figure out how they work?

> *Their hands duely plied the eternal task.*
>
> *The loaded distaff in the left hand placed*
>
> *with spongy coils of snow-white wool was graced.*
>
> *From these the right hand lengthy fibers drew*
>
> *which into thread 'neath nimble fingers grew.*

> *At intervals a gentle touch was given*
>
> *by which the twirling whorl was onward driven.*
>
> *Then when the sinking spindle reached the ground,*
>
> *the new-made thread around the spire was wound.*

5) These are whorls.

On which tool will you find the whorl?

Identify it on the illustration above.

Do you think a whorl needs to be heavy, or should it be light? Why?

1

Discussion: The pictures on this page will help you see how the distaff and spindle are used. Which is the distaff, which the spindle, and where is the whorl?

Name other objects that you think mostly women use or have used in the past. Have men sometimes used these objects too?

What objects have mostly men used in the past? Have women sometimes used these objects too?

Handspinning Activity

To make yarn from wool by using a drop spindle you:

- place about 15 inches of rough, hairy wool in something that can hold it like a distaff.
- pull some strands from the wool, twisting them with your fingers to make yarn.
- tie this yarn to a spindle with a hook, or groove on the shaft, about 1/2 inch above the whorl.
- wind the yarn up the spindle shaft clockwise, securing it under the hook or in the groove at the top.
- pull a tuft of wool from the distaff with your left hand, holding the very end between your thumb and first finger. Overlap it unto the yarn on the spindle.
- give the spindle a sharp twist to the right with your right hand. This will spin the spindle in the air like a top spins on the ground.
- while spinning the spindle twist the yarn with your right fingers.
- with your left hand, draw out some more of the wool. The fibres being pulled down from the distaff form a triangle leading into the spun yarn. Each time you have made a few draws downward, give the spindle a twist now and then so it keeps spinning downward.
- when you have a length of yarn spun, wind it on the spindle body. Build the yarn into a cone shape.

Hand Spinning takes practice. For best results, contact your local weaving store for advice or have a local weaver come to class to demonstrate the technique.

You may write to the following sources for detailed instructions:

1) Ilios: Living History for the Classroom: Box 2723, Liverpool, New York, 13090. This resource sells a guide explaining how to hand spin, ***Hands On Spinning,*** plus wool, wool cards, and drop spindles.

2) Clemes & Clemes Spinning Wheels, 650 San Pablo Avenue, Pinole, CA 94564. Ask for the booklet, ***The Complete Guide to Hand Spinning*** by K. Grasset.

Women of Pompeii - Women of Athens

If Cornelia had lived about 500 years earlier in the city of Athens in Greece her life would have been much more restricted. The following is a list of laws which regulated the lives of women who were citizens in Athens. Using information from the story, put a check next to those laws that Cornelia would **not** have had to obey in Pompeii.

In Athens Women Who Were Citizens Could Not....

_____ Vote

_____ Leave their homes to be seen in public except for religious events

_____ Be in a business in which they made a lot of money

_____ Be in government

_____ Be in professions like medicine, law or the theater

_____ Marry without the consent of a guardian when they were young

_____ Own property

_____ Go to school

The following are some Roman laws that describe rights women did and did not have in Pompeii. Put a check next to those that are similar to rights women have or do not have today in the United States.

In Pompeii Women Could...

_____ Own property

_____ Go to school

_____ Receive an inheritance

_____ Get a divorce

_____ Own a business

In Pompeii Women Could Not...

_____ Marry a foreigner

_____ Marry without the consent of a guardian

_____ Be in government

_____ Serve in the army

What rights did Cornelia have that women in Athens did not have?

_____

_____

_____

What restrictions applied to women in both cities?

_____

_____

_____

Research: Find the answers to these questions.

In the United States women...

1) Won the right to vote in _____.

2) Won the right to own property in _____.

3) Have the right of guardianship over their children.   ____ Yes   ___ No

---

"There are numerous actions decent by our standards which are thought base [by the Greeks]. For what Roman is ashamed to take his wife to a dinner-party? Where does the lady of the house not occupy the place of honor, and receive guests? This is all very different in Greece: she is only invited to dinners of the family and sits only in the inner part of the house, which is called the women's quarters; no one enters unless bound by ties of kinship."
  - from *Lives of the Foreign Generals*

A Woman Speaks Out:
Hortensia's Speech to the Roman Forum

In 42 B.C. Hortensia, a noble woman, was one of 1,400 wealthy women who were taxed to pay the expenses of civil wars (wars between citizens of the same country) which were disrupting the Roman Republic. The women feared that taxes collected from them might be used in battles against their families.

Hortensia led a group of women into the Forum in Rome. Women were not allowed to speak here. Nevertheless, Hortensia did speak up and stated the case of women who felt unfairly taxed. The following are some of the arguments she used in her speech:

"If you take away our property, you will reduce us to a condition unsuitable to our birth, our way of life, and our female nature."

"Why should we pay taxes when we do not share in the office, honors, military commands, nor, in short, the government, for which you fight between yourselves with such harmful results? You say 'because it is wartime.' When have there not been wars?"

"When have taxes been imposed on women, whom nature sets apart from all men?"

"Our mothers once went beyond what is natural and made a contribution during the war against the Carthaginians, when danger threatened your entire empire and Rome itself. But then they contributed willingly, not from their landed property, their fields, their dowries, or the houses...but only from their jewelry."

"Let war with the Celts or Parthians come, we will not be inferior to our mothers when it is a question of common safety. But for civil wars, may we never contribute nor aid you against each other."

The Roman leaders were angry with the women for daring to hold a public meeting and for objecting to contributing money when men had to serve in the army. The crowd, however, supported the women and the leaders reduced the number of women subject to taxation to 400.

Read the speech sentence by sentence and discuss the meaning of each argument. Then answer these questions.

1) The women did not want to be taxed because:

• heavy taxes would take away their _____

• they did not have a part in _____

• they felt that women's nature was different from _____ nature.

• the wars fought were not against foreign invaders, like the Celts, but against

_____

2) When were the women willing to be taxed? _____

_____

3) Would a poor woman be able to make this speech? _____

Restate the argument that shows that Hortensia spoke for wealthy women.

_____

4) Would a man make this speech? _____

Restate an argument that shows that Hortensia spoke for Roman women.

_____

_____

Research: Find a speech by a woman in United States history who spoke out, such as Mother Jones, Anne Hutchinson, Soujourner Truth, and so on. Read parts of the speech aloud in class and explain why the woman gave it.

Creative writing: Make up a speech about an issue women in the United States might debate, for example:

• Should women be combatants in war?

• Should women be paid lower wages than men if the work they do is different than the work men do?

• Should businesses provide daycare for working families?

Women of Pompeii
Background Information

In August A.D. 79, Mt. Vesuvius erupted for three days covering the prosperous commercial town of Pompeii with volcanic matter, ashes and mud. Eventually its fate was forgotten and Pompeii lay buried for nineteen centuries. Now it is revealed as a prime example of a typical small cosmopolitan Roman port town of between 10 - 20 thousand people. Pompeii's extensive and well preserved buildings, paintings, mosaics, artifacts and writings (graffiti) on its walls can tell us much about Roman life in the first century A.D.

Classes of Women: Since most people were *slaves,* the bulk of the female population was enslaved. Female slaves were used primarily in household tasks, although some became midwives, actresses, hairdressers, and prostitutes. There is mention of a female doctor in Pompeii. Doctors, architects, engineers, teachers, and actors all were mostly slave-held professions and were held in low regard by the Romans. The children of the slaves were either kept in the household, sold, or exposed at birth. Marriage between slaves was not legal. In spite of this slaves contracted their own form of marriage. Both men and women could eventually buy their freedom or have it granted to them in a manumission ceremony.

Many *freedwomen* lived as poorly as the slaves. Denied the luxuries of the upper classes, they lived in cramped homes or apartments and got their water from the public fountain. Some freedwomen became business people and a few even became wealthy. It was from this class and the *plebeian* class that most female shopkeepers and artisans came.

Often plebeian and freedwomen worked in textile manufacturing or did laundry work. Women also worked at the mills, where grain was ground; others were landladies, or sold or hawked foods. One owned a brick-making business; another was a money lender. In Pompeii, Eumachia, from a successful brick making family, became very successful and displayed her wealth by donating to the amphitheater and small theater and by building the Fuller's Guild on the forum. She also erected an imposing tomb for herself.

Women of the *equites* (higher status businesspeople) and *patrician* classes had many competent slaves and had the time and money to lavish on themselves. They adorned themselves in the bright colored hanging gown (stola) and wrap (palla), which indicated to the world their citizenship and rank. They also wore elaborate hairdos and makeup. They lived in relative comfort in beautiful houses decorated with murals or mosaic frescoes. These paintings often depicted the lives of local people, like the realistic scene in **Nothing Lasts Forever** which illustrates an

1

initiation ceremony into the Dionysus cult. This mural is found in the "Villa of Mysteries," an estate just outside Pompeii.

Wealthy women, nevertheless, were expected to manage the house, supervise the slaves, and do their own spinning and weaving. Although Roman women were not secluded like women in Athenian Greece, there were separate women's quarters in well-to-do homes, and separate women's sections at the public baths. Kitchens tended to be dark and small and tucked away in the less public parts of the house.

Females who were citizens were educated at home if they were wealthy, and at public school through the elementary level if they were less well off. Women were expected to hold their own in conversations at dinners, festivals, and at the theater.

Women and Religion: The Romans believed in many gods and goddesses. Much of women's time was spent performing necessary rituals to the household and official gods. Cults from the East were popular with women as they offered an emotional outlet that women could not find in the official state cults. For example, the cult of Isis, which originated in Egypt, promised resurrection after death and offered women equal status with men. Isis also was a wife and mother and had lost a child. She thus appealed to women and men who saw in her a mother figure. Worshippers in these cults often underwent secret initiation rites which included trances, feasting, and dancing. Some, such as the Bona Dea festivals, were only for women.

Rights of Women: In early Rome the power of the father (pater familia) was all. In the Law of the Twelve Tablets it stated that the father had to raise all his sons, but needed to raise only one daughter. Throughout this early period, girls were put out

to die at birth more frequently than boys and, in childhood, were given less to eat than boys. Roman women could not vote, hold public office, serve on juries, nor plead in court. In law, women were subject to the guardianship of their father and then their husband. They were not allowed to administer their own affairs, nor did they have the right, until later, of guardianship of their own children.

Some laws regarding women's status became more lenient over time. For example, a freer form of marriage replaced the older form (in manu). Free marriage introduced the concept of marriage as a free and dissoluble union of two equal partners. With it the father did not transfer the manus, or hand, of his daughter to her husband. The father therefore could retained control over the daughter's property. Divorce was easier to attain since after a divorce the family could still manage their daughter's affairs. In order to counter a decrease in population, after Augustus a law was passed allowing women who had three children absolute independence in the management of their personal property. For several centuries a large proportion of women qualified for, and probably availed themselves of, this legal privilege, especially after all residents of the empire were made citizens in 212. Women, mainly urban propertied women, held perhaps 25 to 40 percent of private property in this later period.

In spite of their limited political power, women had indirect ways to influence politics. Groups of women did gather on occasions to publicly express their feelings, as the Hortensia activity shows. And some imperial women, such as Livia, Agrippina the Younger, or Julia Domna, exercised significant political influence during their "reign."

Wall painting from a first century C.E. house in Pompeii.
(The writing implement and tablets she holds and the manuscript
scroll he holds show they are well to do people of learning.)

Selected Bibliography

Antti Arjava, **Women and Law in Late Antiquity**, Oxford Press, 1996.

J.P.V.D. Balsdon, **Roman Women: Their History and Habits**, Harper & Row, 1962.

Elizabeth Wayland Barber, **Women's Work: The First 20,000 Years, Women, Cloth, and Society in Early Times**, W.W. Norton & Company, 1994.

Richard A. Bauman, **Women and Politics in Ancient Rome**, Routledge, 1992.

Sara Bisel, **The Secrets of Vesuvius: Exploring the Mysteries of an Ancient Buried City,** The Madison Books, 1993. A female archeologist helps excavate Herculaneum. Middle School.

Peder Foss, "Kitchens and Dining Rooms at Pompeii; the spatial and social relationship of cooking to eating in the Roman household,' Ph.D. thesis, University of Michigan, Web Document, DIOTIMA, 1994.

Norma Lorre Goodrich, **Priestesses**, HarperCollins, 1990.

Diana Kleiner and Sue Matheson, editors, **I Claudia II: Women in Roman Art and Society**, University of Texas Press, 2000. Specialists look at lives of women as revealed in Roman art.

Mary R. Lefkowitz and Maureen B. Fant, **Women's Life in Greece & Rome: A Source Book in Translation**, The Johns Hopkins University Press, 1982.

Michael Massey, **Women in Ancient Greece & Rome**, Cambridge University Press, 1988. Young Adult.

Sarah B. Pomeroy, **Goddesses, Whores, Wives, and Slaves, Women in Classical Antiquity**, Schochen Books, 1975.

B. Rawson,ed., **The Family in Ancient Rome,** 1986.

Zinserling, Verena, **Women in Greece and Rome,** Abner Schram, 1973.

See the complete Women In World History Curriculum catalog on the Internet at: www.WomenInWorldHistory.com

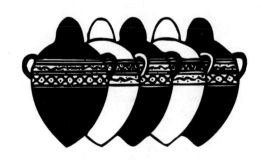